John Minihan's
CORK

John Minihan's
CORK

ROBERT HALE • LONDON

ISBN 0 7090 7714 9

Robert Hale Limited
Clerkenwell House
Clerkenwell Green
London EC1R 0HT

A catalogue record for this book is available from the British Library

2 4 6 8 10 9 7 5 3 1

Printed and bound in China by Midas Printing International Limited

Contents

Dedicated to
Sonia Minihan
1954–2003

Foreword

John Minihan is one of the most remarkable photographers of his time. There is a unique quality about his work that is at once startling and classic, a combination that appears naturally to belong rather than to be there for effect. Repeatedly in Minihan's photography the camera's comment is missing. Instead, something is simply happening. And the more strikingly that seems to be so the more what you're looking at seems to be art.

Newspapers became John Minihan's world when he was hardly more than a child. Born in Dublin and brought up for the early years of his life in Athy, Co. Kildare, he was taken to London when his family emigrated in 1957. In time he was employed as a runner for the *Daily Mail*, making tea, taking wire photographs to the darkroom to be copied, and eventually apprenticed as a photographic printer. Later he became the youngest staff photographer on the *Evening Standard*, and has never since underestimated the role photojournalism played in his life for the next forty years.

There are glimpses of that gritty influence in the insistent urgency of many Minihan photographs, no matter what the subject or how casual the occasion. There is an importance which, again, is not contrived, its presence neither sought nor pressed and there is affection – for the craft, for the camera, and often for the subject. The mysterious is also an element; I doubt very much Minihan knows how he does it.

Vulnerable, shy, yet clearly happier than when she became a princess, Lady Diana Spencer is in the company of two small children who share unease with her. Her see-through dress reveals more than she knew it would, which is what has made the photograph as renowned as the image of Marilyn Monroe in disarray above an air vent. Both pictures deal in human frailty, but Minihan tells more, more stylishly, and more subtly.

That photograph was taken in the autumn of 1980. In 1980, too, Minihan for the first time was permitted to photograph Samuel Beckett and five years later he produced his almost legendary study of the playwright at the Café de Paris, two empty coffee cups and an ashtray of butts in the foreground. In the later 1980s there were Francis Bacon, William Burroughs and plenty more of Beckett, but Minihan's Irish roots had been periodically visited, and continued to be: to record the town of Athy and its people, and to create in particular *The Wake of Katy Tyrrell*, probably the most extraordinary photographic sequence ever inspired by a familiar Irish custom.

In the portraits that have accumulated – before that time and since it – the fastidious reveal themselves, as the worried do, and the easy-going and the reticent, as the bustling extrovert does, and the odd poseur. In a gesture caught, an eyebrow raised, a scowl, a smile, truth is drawn from the depths – and painlessly, as Burroughs observed, for Minihan is the kindest of operators.

But words can be obtrusive. County Cork has long been another Minihan fascination and here it is.

William Trevor

Artists

John Kingerlee, English abstract artist, photographed in 2002 in the Beara Peninsula, an area much favoured by artists, and where he has spent most of his working life.

Frank Russell, celebrated American artist and art historian, photographed in his studio near Kilcrohane in 2001. His seminal work on Picasso's 'Guernica' received international acclaim.

Tim Goulding, well-known abstract Modern Irish artist. A member of *Aosdana*, an affiliation of distinguished artists and writers. He has lived and worked on the Beara Peninsula since 1969.

Cormac Boydell, artist and sculptor based at Allihies on the Beara Peninsula photographed in 2004. Formerly a geologist, he is one of Ireland's foremost artists working in clay.

Charles Tyrrell, well-known Meath-born abstract painter, who exhibits in Dublin, Cork and London and has represented Ireland in several international exhibitions, photographed in 2001 in Allihies in the Beara Peninsula, where he has lived for twenty years.

Susan O'Toole, well-known painter and sculptor, photographed in front of one of her installations in 2001. She is a long-term West Cork resident.

Francis Humphries, founder of the West Cork Chamber Music Festival, photographed in 2000 at Bantry House with the celebrated Irish artist, Bill Crozier.

Brian Lalor, artist–writer and general editor of the *Encyclopaedia of Ireland*, photographed in 1998 at the West Cork Arts Centre in Skibbereen.

John Philip Murray, Dublin-born, Cork-based artist, photographed in his studio in Macroom in 2004.

Ken Thompson, sculptor and stonemason, photographed in his studio in Ballycotton in 2001. He is a specialist in ecclesiastical work and famous for his sculpture at the Air India Disaster Memorial Garden at Ahakista.

Hammond Journeaux, New Zealand-born artist photographed in 2003 in Ballydehob, where she lives.

Pat Connor, Dublin-born artist, photographed at the West Cork Arts Centre in Skibbereen in 1998. He is a long-term resident of Schull.

Writers

Group of Cork poets outside the Long Valley, a well-known literary pub in Cork City in 2000. *Left to right:* Liz O'Donoghue, Theo Dorgan, Gerry Murphy, Trevor Joyce, Rosemary Canavan, Patrick Galvin, Gregory O'Donoghue.

Neil Jordan, film director and writer, who spends part of the year at his house on the Beara Peninsula. London, 1987.

Denise Hall, writer and journalist, photographed with one of her ponies called Percy, in Glengarriff in 1999.

John Montague, internationally famous poet, photographed with Charles Haughey, former Irish Prime Minister in Dublin 1997. He is a long-term Ballydehob resident.

Patrick Galvin, Cork-born poet and dramatist, author of 'Mad Women of Cork', photographed in Cork City in 1997.

Hugo Hamilton, writer, with Mary Johnson, organiser of the Munster Literary Festival and Evelyn Conlon, novelist, photographed leaving the Granary Theatre in Cork in 1988.

Samuel Menashe, American poet and resident of New York City, photographed in Schull after a reading in 1999.

Jenny Joseph, English poet, frequent visitor to West Cork, photographed in 1998.

John Montague, poet, and John Calder, publisher, photographed in a country lane near Schull in 1998.

Eamonn Sweeney, highly regarded Irish literary novelist, photographed in Skibbereen in 2004.

Wolf Mankowitz, English novelist, short-story writer, screenwriter and director, who lived in Ahakista for over thirty years, photographed there in 1997.

Bernard O'Dongohue, Cork-born poet and Professor of Medieval English at the University of Oxford, photographed in London in 1997.

Billy Collins, American Poet Laureate in 2001, photographed in Eyeries on the Beara Peninsula in 2001. He conducts annual workshops in Castletownbere.

Patrick Galvin, poet (*left*), photographed in Cork City in 1997, with Glen
Patterson, Belfast-born poet.

Victoria Glendinning, distinguished English-born biographer and long-term West Cork resident, photographed in Skibbereen in 1998.

William Trevor, photographed in 1982. He is described by the *New Yorker* as, 'Probably the greatest living writer of short stories in the English language'. He was born in Mitchelstown, Co. Cork.

Desmond O'Grady, Limerick-born poet, educated at University College Dublin and Harvard. He lived in Paris, where he knew Samuel Beckett, and later in Italy, where he befriended Ezra Pound. Photographed in 1991 in Kinsale, where he now lives.

Patrick Skene-Catling, English-born novelist, journalist and famous boulevardier. He has lived in Ahakista for over thirty years. Photographed at the Hugh Lane Gallery in Dublin at the Francis Bacon Studio installation in 2001.

Maurice Riordan, Cork-born poet, now based in London, photographed
outside the Cork Arts Theatre in 2001.

Padraic Fiacc, Belfast-born, American-educated poet, whose later work has dealt with the horrors of politcal violence, photographed in 1998 after a reading in Toormore.

John Heath-Stubbs, English poet (*left*), photographed near Ballydehob in 1997 with Ulick O'Connor, Dublin-born man of letters.

Erik Christian Haugaard, Danish-born writer and translator of Hans Christian Andersen, photographed at his home in Ballydehob, where he has lived for many years.

Aidan Higgins, Kildare-born novelist and short story writer, photographed with his wife Alannah Hopkin, the writer and journalist, in Kinsale in 1988.

Stan Gebler-Davies, writer and journalist, who died in Dublin in 1994. London-based for most of his career, he lived latterly in Kinsale, where this photograph was taken in 1984.

Cathal O'Searcaigh, Donegal-born Irish language poet, photographed after a reading at University College Cork in 1998.

Marie Heaney, writer and wife of poet Seamus Heaney, photographed at the Crawford Municipal Art Gallery, Cork City, in 1998.

Roddy Doyle, Booker prize-winning Dublin novelist, photographed at Bantry House in 2003 after participating in the West Cork Literary Festival.

Kenzie Monrad, French novelist, photographed in Durrus in 2001.

Robert O'Donoghue, poet and former literary editor of the *Irish Examiner*, photographed in Cork City in 1998.

Religion

The Church of Ireland church at Farahy, where Elizabeth Bowen, novelist, worshipped and was buried. The photograph, taken in 1999, shows the lectern, where the names of the Bowen family are carved.

St Finbarre's Church of Ireland Cathedral in Cork City photographed in 2004.

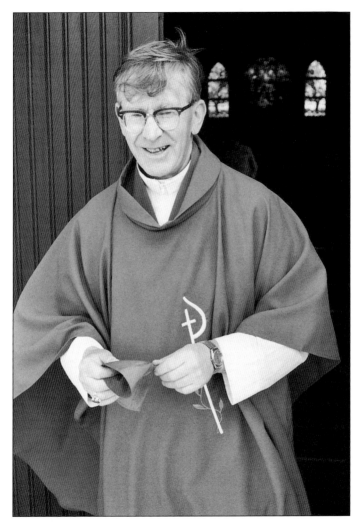

The Most Reverend John Buckley, Roman Catholic Bishop of Cork and Ross photographed meeting parishioners after Mass at St Brigid's Church in Ballydehob in 2000.

The Right Reverend Paul Colton, Church of Ireland Bishop of Cork, Cloyne and Ross, meeting parishioners outside St Finbarre's Cathedral on Easter Sunday 2004.

Hilary Wakeman, Canon of the Church of Ireland, at Altar Church, Toormore, in 1998.

Altar girls outside Skibbereen Cathedral in 2002 waiting to lead the procession at the start of the First Holy Communion mass.

The chapel of the Convent of the Sisters of Mercy, Skibbereen, in 2003. The convent closed in 2003 after 143 years.

Father Joseph Spillane celebrating the mass known as 'the Stations' in a private house near Ballydehob in 2001. 'The Stations' originated in penal times, when Roman Catholics had to worship secretly.

A Corpus Christi procession passing along the main street in Ballydehob in 1998.

Sister Juanita from the Peru Mission taking a photograph of the last remaining Sisters of Mercy in Skibbereen in 2003.

The annual August Mass in 2000 at the Holy Shrine near Bantry, where mass was celebrated in secret in penal times.

Famous famine graveyard at Abbeystrewery near Skibbereen in 2000.

St Barrahane's Church, Castletownshend, where Edith Somerville often played the organ at morning service. Photographed in 1999.

Cork People

Margaret Warren, Texas-born aviatrix, who qualified as a pilot in 1929, photographed in 1998. She is a resident of Castletownshend.

Garret FitzGerald, former Leader of the Fine Gael party and Prime Minister, photographed at Gubbeen House, Schull in 1999.

Jeremy Irons, actor and owner of a fifteenth-century castle at Kilcoe near Ballydehob, photographed at Bantry House in 2001.

Gerald Goldberg, solicitor and former Lord Mayor of Cork, who died aged 92 in December 2003, photographed in his library in Cork in 1999.

Bertie Ahern, Irish Prime Minister, meeting local people, while election-eering in Patrick Street, Cork in 2002.

Conor Lovett, Cork-born actor, distinguished for his performances in Samuel Beckett's plays. Ballydehob, 1998.

Daphne Pocin-Mould, English-born writer and traveller, who has lived in County Cork for over forty years. Ballydehob, 1999.

Theo Dorgan, Cork-born poet and broadcaster, Kent Station, Cork, 1988.

Dr Colin Campbell, English geologist and traveller. Ballydehob, 2004.

Patrick Bergin, Dublin-born Hollywood film star, photographed reading a poem by W.B. Yeats at a concert in Mill Street in 1997.

Peter Murray, Director of the Crawford Municipal Art Gallery. Cork, 2001.

Tom Collins, Skibbereen firefighter with his newly born son Michael. Skibbereen, 2003.

Richard Daly, cobbler, photographed in his workshed. Ballydehob, 1997.

George Sullivan, local historian and ex-miner. Ballydehob, 1998.

The Gabriel Rangers, first ever all-women Gaelic football champions, photographed on St Patrick's Day, 2004, in Skibbereen.

The Bantry Gunners, junior soccer team photographed in Drinagh, Co. Cork in 2004.

Sheep-shearing competition in Balleylickey in 2001.

Annual Christmas Day charity swim, Schull Harbour, 2002.

Fiona Shaw, Cork-born, London-based actress, photographed performing in Samuel Beckett's *Footfalls* in the Garrick Theatre, London, in 1994.

Landscape and Places

Tomcat with his catch of the day. Ballydehob, 1998.

Group of swans in Skibbereen in 1999.

Horse-drawn carriage outside the Metropole Hotel, Cork City in 1976.

Drishane House, Castletownshend, the home of Edith Somerville, co-author with Martin Ross (her cousin Violet Martin) of *Some Experiences of an Irish R.M.*, photographed in 2004.

Ken Thompson's memorial sculpture at the Air India Disaster Garden in Ahakista, 2003.

The grounds of Drishane House, Castletownshend, 2004.

The Eccles hotel, Glengarriff, whose former guests have included such people as Alfred, Lord Tennyson, George Bernard Shaw and the Duke of Windsor.

The famous twelve-arched railway bridge at Ballydehob photographed in 1996. It was part of the now defunct Schull–Skibbereen Railway.

Yachts berthed at Kinsale Harbour, a well-known international yachting venue, 2003.

Vintage tractors taking part in the St Patrick's Day Parade in Skibbereen in 2004.

Rossbrin Harbour, Ballydehob, 1999.

Façade of the Mercy Hospital in Cork City taken in 2000. Originally founded by nuns, it is still one of Cork City's best hospitals.

Cedar tree at Dereenatra, Schull, 1997.

Sculptures at the Crawford Municipal Art Gallery, Cork City, photographed in 2002.

Holiday home of the French film maker, Sophie Toscan du Plantier. The cross marks the spot where she was murdered on 23 December 1996. Schull, 2001.

Bowen's Court, home of the novelist Elizabeth Bowen, which was demolished in the early 1960s.

Musicians

Rory Gallagher, legendary Blues guitarist, photographed at Cork Opera House in Cork City in 1987. He died in 1995.

Shane McGowan, singer and songwriter, formerly of the Pogues, photographed in a recording studio in Bantry in 2001.

Master Class students rehearsing at the West Cork Music Festival at Bantry House in 1999.

The Chieftains, internationally renowned Traditional Irish Music band, photographed at a concert in Mill Street in 1999.

Pecker Dunne, Irish piper, formerly of the Bothy band, photographed in Ballydehob in 2001.

Paddy Keenan, musician and songwriter, famous for his song 'Sullivan John', photographed in McCarthy's Bar in Baltimore in 1981.

Noel Redding, musician, formerly bass guitarist with the Jimi Hendrix Experience, resident in Clonakilty for thirty years until his death in 2003, photographed at De Barra's Bar in Clonakilty in 2000.

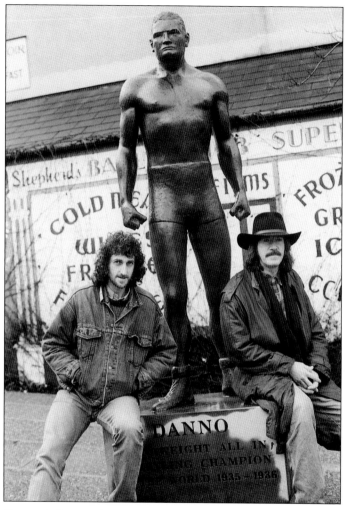

Tommy Sullivan and Paddy Keenan, musicians, photographed sitting by the statue of Danno O'Mahony, 1930s American wrestling champion, in Ballydehob in 2001.

Food

Skibbereen Agricultural Show, 1998.

Prominent members of the Slow Food Movement at Gubbeen House, Schull, in 1999 with the former Irish Prime Minister, Garret FitzGerald. *Left to right*: Annie Barry, Sally Barnes, Bill Hogan, Giana Ferguson, Myrtle Allen, Garret FitzGerald and Darina Allen.

Carlo Petrini, Italian founder of the Slow Food Movement, photographed on his visit to Jeffa Gill of Durrus Farmhouse Cheese, Durrus 2004.

Children competing in the annual Pancake Race in St Brigid's National
School in Ballydehob in 1997.

Organic vegetable grower displaying his produce at Skibbereen Farmers' Market 2003.